"The principles in this book will benefit anyone who wants to do more than dream about life's adventures."

John Goddard, recipient of Encyclopedia Britannica Achievement in Life Award. First explorer to kayak the length of the Nile river.

"A cast of real and imaginary people bring the power tools of personal change to the reader. An entertaining book that shows you how to travel first class and have the life of your dreams."

Lynn Berardo, Editor, *Bay Area Parent Magazine*, California

"I'm ready to hop aboard! I wish I had the *Goal Express!* thirty years ago."

Cybill Shepherd, actress

"For the past five years I've used the techniques in *Goal Express!* My accomplishments have taken leaps and bounds, from traveling, learning, being happy, and doing great in school."

Mike Raffaeli, college student

"My son read it with me. We enjoyed it immensely. The person who puts the ideas of *Goal Express!* into action will almost certainly have a rich, full life, and won't look back wistfully some day and sigh, 'I wish I had....' "

Judith Lipsett, Managing Editor, *OUR KIDS magazine*, Texas

"Truly inspiring. The perfect book to start your own journey as your life is taking shape."

Teyara Gamble, 17

"*Goal Express!* represents a true gift. It is a step-by-step plan promoting self worth through goal setting and personal achievement. Best of all, the ideas . . . are suprisingly easy to recall. . . "

Teresa Hershberger, *Gulf Coast Parent Newspaper*, Florida

"It's fast and to the point, an easy read that specifically shows how to identify and realize those dreams which seem unattainable. It should be required reading in the middle schools. It has the potential to get adolescents grounded in a positive and creative way."

Sherry Glueck, parent education coordinator

"Even now I find myself using your ideas and writing down some of the experiences that I want to accomplish in my lifetime."

Karen Bender, Editor, *Kids N Stuff Magazine*, Florida

"For kids who don't know the color of their parachute. A can-do kind of book that will help youngsters focus on their future."

Cynthia Roberts, Publisher, *Parents Express*, Philadelphia

"*Goal Express!* could be the most important book you'll ever give your child."

Mary Brence Martin, Managing Editor, *Bay Area Parent Magazine*, California

Goal Express!

The Five Secrets of Goal-Setting Success

Jim Wiltens

Deer Crossing Press
Sunnyvale, California

Library of Congress Catalog Card Number: 93–74791: $9.95 Pbk

ISBN 0-938525-06-9

First Printing 1995

Deer Crossing Press
P.O. Box 60517
Sunnyvale, CA 94088-0517

Printed in the United States of America

Dedication

Spun wisps of thought

woven on mental looms

create patterns called reality,

the fabric of our lives.

Whether sackcloth or silk,

the choice is always ours.

To all those who helped me understand it was a choice.

• • • • •

While I have practiced and taught the five secrets of successful goal-setting for decades, I still experience a sense of wonder and joy each time I turn a dream into reality.

When designing the cover for *Goal Express!*, my goal was to have a realistic image of a fantastical train. This was accomplished by constructing the train from an array of discarded house hold items. The parts list includes an iron, alarm clock, lamp, parts from a computer, lock, plumbing fixtures, Christmas tree ornaments, pulleys, radio speakers, and other junk yard gems.

Not having the background or tools of a model builder, the train posed numerous creative challenges. Yet each of these challenges was overcome by concentrating on the goal-setting process. Especially helpful were the *bridging questions* covered in Chapter 5.

Books by Jim Wiltens

Individual Tactics in Water Polo

Thistle Greens and Mistletoe: Edible and Poisonous Plants of Northern California

No More Nagging, Nit-picking, & Nudging: A Guide to Motivating, Inspiring, and Influencing Kids Aged 10-18

Goal Express! The Five Secrets of Goal-Setting Success

TABLE OF CONTENTS

Turning Dreams Into Reality

I should have seen it coming.

Teens in my goal-setting class were listening to me describe how you turn dreams into reality. I was at the point where I explain the importance of writing goals in a blank paged book. As each aspiration is recorded, this blank book is transformed into a personal catalog of goals. I call it a dream book.

One student raised his hand and asked, "What are some goals in your dream book?"

I innocently opened my dream book and read off several entries. Goals like purchasing a home and being able to remember the names of ten people at a party were real yawners for my teenage audience. But they perked up when I read, "Become a nationally published cartoonist." Now, that was cool. The only thing better might have been rock star or astronaut. This goal prompted several more questions. One of those questions was, "Are you, like, an artist?"

"No," I replied, "but I did a lot of doodling in the margins of my notes in high school."

I think this admission of novice status sealed my fate.

"Yo, Jim. You're telling us all this stuff about how we can turn *our* dreams into reality. How about we see *you* turn a dream into reality?" The students looked at me expectantly. "Become a nationally published cartoonist."

"Um, yeah, aaahhh, I'll think about it," was my reply. For a week I mulled over the possibilities. It wouldn't be easy. But most big dreams aren't. I then started a familiar goal-setting process. By the next class I was ready with my reply: "I'll do it." I think they were surprised. Within a year, I sold cartoons to such national magazines as *SKI* and *Black Belt Magazine.* I had so much fun with this goal, I went on to illustrate two books and publish cartoons in numerous publications including the *San Francisco Chronicle, Sources, COMDEX,* and *Bay Area Parent Magazine.*

Whether you want to become a cartoonist, a cardiologist, a carpenter, or a candlestick maker, goal setting is the way. Using goal-setting techniques, I've become an author, held a killer whale in my arms, co-founded a children's summer camp, earned a black belt in the martial arts, married a wonderful woman, kayaked wild jungle rivers, started a professional speaking career, and prepared sushi. New experiences, self-confidence, knowledge, and friendships are all fringe benefits of the goal-setting process. But one of the greatest rewards for me has been a sense of control over my destiny. Knowing where you want to go and how to get there is a wonderful feeling. You too can have this feeling.

This Is Your Invitation

You can turn your dreams into reality. This book is your invitation for a ride on an unusual locomotive — the *Goal Express!* Most of the passengers you are about to meet are real people, a few aren't. All the characters, whether whimsical or factual, will show you how you can reach your destination.

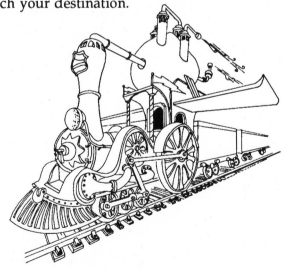

All Aboard!

Arriving at the train station you notice a dense crowd milling around outside. They all want to ride the *Goal Express!*, but the entrance to the station eludes them. They don't know where to begin. To get through this meandering crowd, you need to purchase a blank book. Get a hardcover book, the kind that will last a lifetime. This is your dream book. It is your ticket. Take a firm grip on your dream book and pass through the crowd into the train station. You are now in the company of thousands of successful travelers who have started their trips from where you are standing right now.

But no time for gawking.

The *Goal Express!* is leaving the station.

ALL ABOARD!

Otto B. Positiff

The porter guides you to your seat. In the seat facing yours is a fellow passenger. He is wearing an immaculate suit, white as vanilla ice cream. His shoes are white, his socks are white, even his tie is starch white — except for a tiny black dot. As you seat yourself, he greets you cheerfully. "Howdy. Name's Otto B. Positiff. My card."

You accept a business card, completely blank — except for a black dot in the center. The opposite side is identical. You look questioningly at Mr. Positiff.

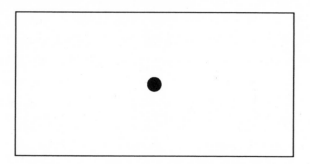

Mr. Positiff leans forward enthusiastically. "What do you see?"

"Why, I see a black dot."

"Haarr, haaarrrr," guffaws Mr. Positiff. "That's what most people say."

"But that's all there is," you reply matter-of-factly.

"Look again," says Mr. Positiff. "You'll notice that 99 percent of the card is white paper. Yet, the first thing you saw was the black dot."

Your face is blank.

"People have a tendency to focus on the black dots in their lives," says Mr. Positiff. "They focus so hard on the blemishes, they miss seeing the white paper. For instance, I know these parents, their child can come home with straight A's and one C minus, and guess which grade the parents dwell on?" Mr. Positiff points at the dot on his card. "Yep, when you concentrate on blotches, you miss the good. A beautiful teenager I know makes excuses for skipping school if she has a couple of pimples. When she looks in the mirror, all she can see are the pimples. This may sound silly, but if you've ever dwelled on lacking something like money, popularity, brains, strength, you name it, then you know all about focusing on the black dots and missing all the white paper. You get my drift?"

"I'm not sure what this has to do with . . . "

"Is that your dream book?"

Your eyes shift to the crisp new dream book on your lap. "Why, yes."

He pulls out a dog-eared volume from his vest pocket. "This here's my dream book. Could be the most important book in my world. You know why?"

You shake your head, no.

"Does two things. First, it is a reminder of the positive things I'm looking forward to. Keeps me focused on all the white paper, you might say." He absentmindedly flips through pages in the book. "Second, over the years it has become a record of dreams I've turned into reality. This is important." Mr. Positiff shifts in his seat. "As a kid I got a lot of pats on the back. It helped build my confidence. But seems as you get older, those pats get fewer and further between. I now give myself a personal pat on the back. Regularly looking through my dream book focuses me on my successes. Concentrating on success gives me the confidence to tackle bigger dreams." He pats the book and slips it back in his vest pocket. He looks at you expectantly.

You nod slowly and put his business card in your pocket.

Betty Buttons

Your conversation is interrupted by the noisy arrival of another passenger. Her outfit is the source of sound. Every square inch of fabric is occupied by two-inch-wide buttons. The kind of buttons that have slogans on them. As she seats herself next to Mr. Positiff, her buttons clack together like castanets.

"Mr. Positiff, what a pleasure," she says.

Mr. Positiff smiles openly. Obviously, they are friends.

You can't help but stare at her bounty of buttons. They have slogans on them such as "Goals are dreams with a time limit," "We are where we are because we have first imagined it," and "Those who do most, dream most."

Your goggle-eyed stare does not go unnoticed.

"It seems quite odd, doesn't it?" she says, looking you directly in the eye.

"Why, yes," you reply.

"Strange indeed. You don't have a single button." She looks over her outfit, unclips a button, and leans across to pin it to your shirt.

"My name is Betty Buttons. My trade is Personal Motivation. I motivate myself."

"How interesting," you reply.

"Yes, it is, isn't it?" Her smile twinkles. "I know we've just met, but I was wondering . . . I noticed you have a dream book in your lap and was curious to know if you'd be willing to participate in an experiment."

"An experiment . . ." you hesitate. "Is it safe?"

"We haven't lost anybody yet," she replies.

"All right."

"Good." She looks over her brocade of buttons and points at one. "What do you see?"

Button #1: The Woman's Face

"A woman's face," you reply.

"Excellent. Now take the button that I gave you earlier and look at it closely."

You remove the button from your shirt and gaze at it intently.

Button #2: The Button In Your Hand

"Why, it's the woman's face."

Ms. Buttons laughs delightedly. "Now, look at this button." She holds up another button.

Button #3: The Dancing Elephant

"It's a dancing elephant."

"Now back up and look at the button in your hand again."

"That's odd. Sometimes button #2 looks like a woman's face, and sometimes it looks like a dancing elephant."

"It's not odd at all. I've simply readjusted your mind filters."

You hold up a hand, "Whoa. I think you lost me on the mind filters."

"Not surprising. Most people aren't aware of their mind filters, but we all have them." Betty taps her head. "Have you ever been to a party and noticed how you can tune out all the other conversations going on around you except the one you want to listen to?"

"Sure," you reply.

"Well, that's an example of mind filtering. You couldn't possibly listen to all the conversations going on at a party, so you select one and filter the others out." Betty pauses. "Our filters are working all the time. There are so many sights, sounds, and feelings coming at us at any one time that we would go crazy if we tried to pay attention to them all. It would be like staring at a brilliant sun. Our mind filters, like sunglasses, let in a limited amount of information and screen out the rest."

Ms. Buttons taps her buttons. "And the experiment we just did shows how you can readjust your filters."

"Readjust my filters?"

"When I showed you the button of the woman's face, I opened your filters for that image. Then I had you look at the button in your hand. Your mind was prepared to let through any information that would enable you to see a woman's face, which it did. Next I showed you a dancing elephant. When you looked at the button in your hand this time, you saw a dancing elephant. Here, take these three buttons and try the experiment on friends. Show your friends either the woman's face or the dancing elephant. The first picture they see will prime them to see that same image in button #2."

"What does this have to do with my dream book?"

Ms. Buttons smiles at Mr. Positiff, who returns a knowing wink.

"What it has to do is this. When you decide on a destination and write it down in your dream book, it will readjust your filters. Information that can help you get to that destination is now more likely to come through."

Ms. Buttons reaches up to tug on one of her earrings. "Have you ever had your ears pierced and suddenly noticed what everyone else is wearing in their pierced ears?" She props a foot on your knee. She's wearing neon red tennis shoes, adorned with Day-Glo buttons. "Or maybe you've bought awesome jock shoes, or a car, or glasses, and suddenly there's a spotlight on anyone else you see who has these same things?"

"Yes."

"That's filter readjustment. Information comes through the sieve because of your new awareness. Most people's filters are tweaked around by circumstances or other people. When you watch commercials on television for something like belly button deodorant or glucose-enriched scooter pies, you've got people working on your filters. They are trying to adjust your filters so you will be more aware of their products on your next visit to the store. Rather than let someone else fiddle with your filters, why not control your own adjustment?"

"I think I understand," you reply. "Let's see if I have this right. Information and opportunities are shining on me all the time. Only part of it gets through because of my filters. I can determine what parts get through by using my dream book to adjust my awareness. Is that it?"

Ms. Buttons and Mr. Positiff turn to each other and shake hands.

Inspiration For A Dream Book

Just then a conductor comes down the aisle calling, "Dream books, dream books, I need to see your dream books." He stops to check each passenger's dream book. When he arrives at your seat, you hand him your dream book. He flips through it expertly.

"Mmmmm, first trip?"

"Yes."

He fishes a large gold watch out of his pocket. "Then I'll have to make a little time for you." He pushes the hands on the watch back from nine o'clock to eight o'clock. "There, that should be enough time," says the conductor. "Do you know where the inspiration for the dream book came from?"

"No."

"Well, you're in luck." He motions you to follow him down the aisle, eventually stopping at a private compartment. As you enter, a blue-eyed, mustachioed man looks up. He is wearing a khaki safari suit and a bushman's hat with zebra trim. "I'd like to introduce John Goddard. The *Los Angeles Times* called him the 'real-life Indiana Jones.' He's been chased by river pirates, lived with primitive tribes in Borneo, piloted an F-111 jet at 1,500 miles per hour, discovered a Mayan temple, and is the first person to kayak the length of the Nile river. He's an amazing man, but I'll let him tell you about the most amazing thing he's done."

"Hello," you say. "What could be more amazing than all of those adventures? The conductor hinted that it had something to do with the inspiration for the dream book."

Goddard nods.

"When I was fifteen," says Goddard, "I was aware that many adults wished they could live their lives over. They waited and waited for their ships to come in, and in the meantime, their piers collapsed. I thought if I could crystallize my ambitions and start working on them early, life wouldn't pass me by. It's like building a raft and rowing out to meet your ship."

Mr. Goddard tugs a backpack out from under his seat. From one of the pockets, he pulls a sheet of paper and hands it to you. "At age fifteen, I took a sheet of legal paper and wrote out 127 goals. I call it my life list."

John Goddard's Life List

(After each success, John Goddard puts a check mark
next to his completed goal.)

Explore:

√ 1. Nile River
√ 2. Amazon River
√ 3. Congo River
√ 4. Colorado River
  5. Yangtze River, China
  6. Niger River
  7. Orinoco River
√ 8. Rio Coco, Nicaragua

Study Primitive Cultures in:

√ 9. Congo
√ 10. New Guinea
√ 11. Brazil
√ 12. Borneo
√ 13. Sudan
√ 14. Australia
√ 15. Kenya
√ 16. Philippines
√ 17. Tanganyika (now Tanzania)
√ 18. Ethiopia
√ 19. Nigeria
√ 20. Alaska

Climb:

  21. Mt. Everest
  22. Mt. Aconcagua, Argentina

√ 23. Mt. McKinley
√ 24. Mt. Huascarán, Peru
√ 25. Mt. Kilimanjaro
√ 26. Mt. Ararat, Turkey
√ 27. Mt. Kenya
  28. Mt. Cook, New Zealand
√ 29. Mt. Popocatepetl, Mexico
√ 30. Matterhorn
√ 31. Mt. Rainier
√ 32. Mt. Fuji
√ 33. Mt. Vesuvius
√ 34. Mt. Bromo, Java
√ 35. Grand Tetons
√ 36. Mt. Baldy, California

General:

√ 37. Carry out careers in medicine and exploration
  38. Visit every country in the world (30 to go)
√ 39. Study Navajo and Hopi Indians
√ 40. Learn to fly a plane
√ 41. Ride horse in Rose Parade

Photograph:

√ 42. Iguaçu Falls, Brazil
√ 43. Victoria Falls, Rhodesia (now Zimbabwe)
√ 44. Sutherland Falls
√ 45. Yosemite Falls
√ 46. Niagara Falls

General

√ 47. Retrace travels of Marco Polo and Alexander the Great

Explore Underwater:

√ 48. Coral reefs of Florida
√ 49. Great Barrier Reef, Australia
√ 50. Red Sea
√ 51. Fiji Islands
√ 52. Bahamas

Visit:

√ 53. Okefenokee Swamp and the Everglades
54. North and South Poles
√ 55. Great Wall of China
√ 56. Panama and Suez Canals
√ 57. Easter Island
√ 58. The Galapagos Islands
√ 59. Vatican City
√ 60. Taj Mahal

√ 61. Eiffel Tower
√ 62. Blue Grotto, Capri
√ 63. Tower of London
√ 64. Leaning Tower of Pisa
√ 65. Sacred Well of Chichen-Itza, Mexico
√ 66. Ayers Rock in Australia
67. River Jordan from Sea of Galilee to Dead Sea

Swim In:

√ 68. Lake Victoria
√ 69. Lake Superior
√ 70. Lake Tanganyika
√ 71. Lake Titicaca, S. America
√ 72. Lake Nicaragua

Experiences and Skills:

√ 73. Become an Eagle Scout
√ 74. Dive in a submarine
√ 75. Land on and take off from an aircraft carrier
√ 76. Fly in a blimp, balloon, and glider
√ 77. Ride an elephant, camel, ostrich, and bronco
√ 78. Skin-dive to 40 feet and hold breath two-

and-a-half minutes

√ 79. Catch a ten-pound lobster and ten-inch abalone

√ 80. Play flute and violin

√ 81. Type fifty words a minute

√ 82. Make a parachute jump

√ 83. Learn water and snow skiing

√ 84. Go on a church mission

85. Follow the John Muir trail

√ 86. Study native medicines and bring back useful ones

√ 87. Bag camera trophies of elephant, lion, rhino, cheetah, cape buffalo, and whale

√ 88. Learn to fence

√ 89. Learn jujitsu

√ 90. Teach a college course

√ 91. Watch a cremation ceremony in Bali

√ 92. Explore depths of the sea

93. Appear in a Tarzan movie

94. Own a horse, chimpanzee, cheetah, ocelot, and coyote (yet to own a chimp or cheetah)

95. Become a ham radio operator

√ 96. Build own telescope

√ 97. Write a book

√ 98. Publish an article in *National Geographic*

√ 99. High jump five feet

√100. Broad jump fifteen feet

√101. Run a five minute mile

√102. Weigh 175 pounds stripped

√103. Perform 200 sit-ups and 20 pull-ups

√104. Learn French, Spanish, and Arabic

105. Study dragon lizards on Komodo Island

√106. Visit birthplace of Grandfather Sorenson in Denmark

√107. Visit birthplace of Grandfather Goddard in England

√108. Ship aboard a freighter as a seaman

109. Read the entire *Encyclopaedia Britannica*

√110. Read the Bible from cover to cover

√111. Read the works of Shakespeare, Plato, Aristotle, Dickens, Thoreau, Rousseau, Hemingway, Twain,

Burroughs, Tolstoy,
Talmage, Emerson,
Longfellow, Keats,
Poe, Bacon, and
Whittier
√ 112. Become familiar
with compositions
of Bach, Beethoven,
Debussy, Ilbert, Lalo,
Mendelssohn,
Milhaud, Ravel,
Rimsky-Korsakov,
Respighi, Verdi,
Rachmaninoff,
Stravinsky, Toch,
Paganini, and
Tchaikovsky
√ 113. Become proficient
in the use of an air-
plane, motorcycle,
tractor, surfboard,
rifle, pistol, canoe,
microscope, lariat,
and boomerang
114. Compose music
√ 115. Play Clair de Lune
on the piano

√ 116. Watch fire-walking
ceremony
√ 117. Milk a poisonous
snake
√ 118. Light a match with
.22 rifle
√ 119. Visit a movie
studio
√ 120. Climb Cheops'
pyramid
√ 121. Become a member
of the Explorers Club
and the
Adventurers' Club
√ 122. Learn to play polo
√ 123. Travel through the
Grand Canyon on
foot and by boat
√ 124. Circumnavigate the
globe
125. Visit the moon
√ 126. Marry and have
children
127. Live to see the
twenty-first century

You spend several minutes looking over the list. "This is an amazing list."

"That list has served as a thread throughout my life," says Mr. Goddard.

"How many of these dreams have you accomplished?" you ask.

"A check mark next to a dream indicates the ones I have completed," replies Mr. Goddard. "At present, I've accomplished 109 of the 127."

The conductor was right. All the stories of crocodiles, climbing mountains like Kilimanjaro, and trekking through such places as the Congo, are probably not as amazing as a fifteen-year-old boy sitting down and writing a list of dreams and then setting out to turn them into reality.

"I think we've taken enough of Mr. Goddard's time," says the conductor, looking at his gold watch.

"But there's much more I would like to ask," you protest.

"That's often the way it is when a new passenger meets Mr. Goddard. But I have other travelers for you to meet. And besides, we need to give Mr. Goddard time to work on his newest dream. At age 69, he is preparing to fly an F-15."

You say goodbye to Mr. Goddard. You think back to what Betty Buttons said earlier, "You can readjust your filters to let in the information you need." Did Mr. Goddard's life list adjust his filters? Is writing down dreams that powerful? As you leave the car, you notice a sign above the door:

> **Trains that go places**
> **have a printed schedule:**
> **WRITE DOWN YOUR DREAMS**

Know Where You Are Going

"On this railroad, we keep track of dreams. It's one way of helping passengers get to their destinations," says the conductor. "I'd like you to meet Michael Raffaeli. Michael started his dream book five years ago when he was still a teen."

Michael's compartment is loaded with luggage. All the stickers on his baggage show he is a regular on the *Goal Express!* With one hand he gives you a firm handshake; with the other he shoves luggage off a seat so you can sit. He flashes a sunshine smile that lights up the car.

"Michael," asks the conductor, "what do you think is the single most important thing you need to reach your destination?"

"If I could teach only one thing about setting goals," muses Michael, "I'd say it is to focus on a specific goal. Get away from the general. For example, it takes four and a half years for the average student to graduate from UC San Diego. With planning, I've worked it out so that I can graduate in three and a half years, a whole year earlier than most students."

The conductor pats Michael on the shoulder. "Michael uses his dream book to focus, especially when he is faced with what he calls 'life's little bummers.' Could you tell us the story?"

"I had to have knee surgery," says Michael. "This meant I couldn't take a summer backpacking job I really wanted. I overcame the setback by accepting my new situation and rearranging my goals. I discovered a field study program and put it down as a goal in my dream book. That fall, I gathered applications, made telephone calls, got information, and wrote and rewrote my application. Of the forty people who applied, thirteen were accepted. I was one of them."

"It turned out to be quite the adventure," says the conductor. "He traveled to Belize in Central America. Mayan guides led Michael's group into a rainforest that receives few visitors."

"At one point, we came to a river," says Michael. "On one side was a limestone wall with a huge cave. We decided to do some caving. One cavern was so high our flashlight beams didn't reach the ceiling. In another chamber we made cave music by tapping on stalagmites and stalactites. Wading through an underground river, we got our biggest surprise. We set off a bat frenzy." Michael pulls out a photo that shows so many bats, you can't see anyone's face in the picture. "We ended up exploring a mile of unmapped cave."

"The dream book has allowed me to accomplish things I might not have set out to do otherwise," says Michael. "All the things I do in goal setting are constantly giving me an edge in school, in getting jobs, and in going on exciting trips. This quarter, I'm on my way to Costa Rica to study rainforest ecology for two months." Michael pauses and looks you straight in the eye: "Get away from the general, know what you want, and pursue it."

"Michael is big on being specific," says the conductor. "He wants you to be very clear about your destination." The conductor reaches for the window shade and pulls it down. Then he pulls back his waistcoat to reveal a three-foot-long gold fountain pen held in a scabbard attached to his belt. With a flourish, he withdraws the pen. Taking a fencer's stance, the conductor slashes a line down the center of the shade.

"What are some of your destinations?" asks the conductor.

"I'd like to be popular," you answer.

With Zorro-like movements, the conductor writes, *I'd like to be popular*. "Please continue," says the conductor. As he writes down your dreams, some go on one side of the line, some on the other. Soon he has written a number of your goals.

"You tell me which ones are general and which ones are specific," says the conductor.

I want to be popular.	I want to be able to remember the names of twenty people I meet at a party.
I want an interesting life.	I want to go SCUBA diving off the Great Barrier Reef in Australia.
I want to have enough money when I retire.	I want to invest $200 a month in an IRA for the next thirty years.
I want an education.	I want to graduate from UC Berkeley with a degree in psychology.
I want to do more than just enough to get by.	I want to enter the science fair at my school.
I want to own nice things.	I want a sunflower garden in my backyard.
I want to be creative.	I want to enter a recipe in the Betty Crocker Cooking Contest.

I want to be in good physical condition.	I want to run three miles without being exhausted.
I want more confidence.	I want to deliver a speech at the Toastmasters club in front of fifty people.
I want to overcome my fears.	I want to go bungee jumping.
I want to save the planet.	I want to plant four trees.
I want to make people happy.	I want to compliment someone at least once a day.

The conductor whips a circle around all the goals in the right-hand column. "These are the specific ones. Being specific about your destination makes it easier for us to take you there," says the conductor. He slides the gold pen back into its scabbard.

Pencil Test

"Let me introduce you to one of our young riders. Susan Gardner's thirteen. She's busy putting some very specific goals in her dream book. I don't want to disturb her. Let's just peek over her shoulder."

Here is what you see.

"Why, she's drawing pictures," you comment.

"We call it the pencil test," says the conductor. "Passengers who have difficulty being specific often find that a picture is worth a thousand words. When you aren't sure if your words are specific or general, try to draw a picture. We have some passengers whose dream books are filled with drawings of what they want."

"See that picture in the lower right-hand corner?" asks the conductor, pointing. "Susan wants to become a white-water kayaker. She started working on the goal a year ago. She's learned ten paddle strokes, rescue techniques, and how to Eskimo roll (a complex manuever that rights a flipped boat). This summer she qualified to go on a three-day lake kayaking trip. She's steadily moving towards the goal represented by her drawing. Not much longer and she'll be on white water."

High-TEC Dreams

"If I wanted to put some dreams in my dream book," you ask, "do you have any suggestions about where I can start?"

"You might try going the high-TEC route."

"High-TEC?"

"Right," says the conductor. " 'T' stands for *things* you want. For instance, the bicycle from *E.T.*, a bonsai redwood tree, or an Appaloosa pony are all possibilities. 'E' stands for *experiences*. For example, you may want to eat licorice ice cream, attend the senior prom at your high school, or go deep sea fishing for marlin in Mexico. 'C' stands for *characteristics* you want to have, such as the ability to wiggle your ears, the ability to communicate in Spanish, or the creativity to see three solutions to every problem. Why not open your dream book and write down some of your specific dreams? Write down two things you want, two experiences you want, and two characteristics you would like to have in your personality."

"It still seems kind of overwhelming," you respond. "I don't know what I want in my future."

The conductor pushes his hat back. "Getting started is more important than making a total future life plan. Start with little goals. What itsy-bitsy, teeny-weeny goal can you put in your book that you can accomplish in one day or one hour? Maybe you could make a recipe from a cookbook, visit a museum in your town, build a model, learn to use a new computer program, pick up a dress pattern, learn to juggle two balls, call a friend you haven't seen in a long time, arrange with a parent to spend a day at work with them, or make it a goal to write down ten goals. Little goals are the best way to get started toward big goals."

The conductor then looks at his watch. "We need to hurry if you're going to meet all the passengers."

Leaving this car, you notice another sign posted above the door. It reads:

Good goals are like railroad tracks — solid:
BE SPECIFIC

Food For Thought

"Where are we headed now?"

"I thought you might want some nourishment," says the conductor, leading you to the dining car. "I'll be back when you're finished." The conductor hurries off.

A bald waiter with a two-foot-long handlebar mustache approaches. Tiny bells at the ends of his mustache make a delightful tinkling sound. Bowing graciously, he motions you to a seat at a large table.

"Ah, gentleperson of discrimination," says the waiter, snapping open a menu. "The menu."

After a little knit-browed concentration, you look hopelessly at the waiter. "This isn't like any menu I've ever seen before."

"Yes, it can be baffling. Might I be of assistance?"

"Please."

Tweaking his mustache the waiter says, "I suggest an entrepreneurial entree, a rare relationship, a gourmet group goal set, and an irresistible inventor."

"It sounds interesting," you reply. "Will it take long?"

The waiter snaps the towel over his arm, "Only a moment." He then proceeds to various tables around the dining car, whispering in the ears of the diners. Some glance toward your table and nod to the waiter. Within minutes he returns with an entourage of seven people. They seat themselves at your table, which no longer seems as large.

An Entrepreneurial Entree

"Let us begin with food for thought," says the waiter. "Allow me to introduce Michael Cookson. He's founder and past president of Aviea Sports. Michael, could you explain how goals nourish your entrepreneurial spirit?"

"In the beginning, I was afraid to write down my goals," says Michael. "They were so ambitious, I was a little afraid of them. The transition occurred when I started Aviea Sports. To start my company, I needed detailed goals on paper so I could go to investors and convince them to put their faith in me.

"One goal I had for Aviea Sports was to develop a line of sporting goods that would help kids have a positive sports experience. The guiding principles behind our products are based on the 'graduated length method' used in skiing. Beginning skiers start with the positive experience of learning on short skis, which are easier to use, and gradually move up to longer skis. I did the same thing with tennis. We designed a racquet with a shorter handle, making it easier for kids to swing. Next we developed our own tennis ball. It's twice the size of a normal tennis ball, which makes it easier to hit. The ball also bounces slower and no higher than the child's waist. Another feature was a whistle in the racquet's strings. When a child swings correctly, it makes a whistle sound, a positive reinforcement to swing correctly.

"Another product was a high-density foam baseball bat with a weight inside. When kids swing the bat, it makes a cracking sound. It teaches a child to swing through to make the sound. It's lighter than a wood or aluminum bat but has enough heft for a child to hit a high-density foam baseball a long way. Kids benefit by hitting far yet are not hurt if the ball hits them.

"Another of our goals was to sell our products in big stores such as Target, K-Mart, and Toys R Us. Now, this may sound like a nothing event, but for a person who has never been in the industry, asking Toys R Us to run a test in their stores was a big thing. In the toy company arena, it was a marketing breakthrough.

"Now I'm a firm believer in putting goals on paper. In just four years, Aviea developed eighteen products. We also exceeded our profit and sales goals. When I sold the company to Mattel, Aviea was grossing forty million dollars a year."

"Michael," asks the waiter, "if you could say only one thing to fledgling entrepreneurs, what would it be?"

After a pause, Michael replies, "I would simply ask, 'What do you want to do?' Strip away layers from what you think you should do and decide what you *want* to do. After getting to the core, I'd say, 'Okay, go find a way to do it.' "

The waiter turns to you. "So what do you want to do? Take that first step in making your dreams real by writing them down."

The waiter taps one of the bells hanging from the end of his mustache. "Now let's make room for a rare relationship. Jim Wiltens and Ellen McNeil have been using a dream book in the four years of their marriage to improve their relationship."

A Rare Relationship

"When Ellen and I decided to get married," says Jim, "I like to think we spent more time planning our lives than planning the wedding. We made it a goal to have a continuing process for finding ways to make our relationship better. We set aside time each month to accomplish this goal."

"We keep track on paper of what we discuss," says Ellen. "For instance, we have what we call the 'Calvin and Margaret' goals. Calvin is the cartoon character who would try anyone's patience. Margaret is the little girl who plagues Dennis the Menace. Like most couples, we know that selfishness or an unwillingness to see things from our partner's viewpoint can damage our relationship. We labeled these behaviors Calvin and Margaret, and we want to minimize the time either of us has to spend with Calvin or Margaret."

"My negative side is represented by Calvin," says Jim. "Ellen gets Margaret."

"We defined behaviors that could damage our relationship," says Ellen. "Then we worked on ways to overcome the Calvin-Margaret cycle. We found it helpful to develop guidelines for dealing with a potential confrontation: first, speak in the present tense; second, do not blame anyone or anything; third, propose a solution that is beneficial to the relationship; and fourth, hug."

"At our meetings, we look for instances where we have met our goals," says Jim. "We record our successes on paper. Being aware of the Calvin-Margaret cycle and setting specific goals to replace this pattern with more positive behaviors have contributed to a positive and happy relationship."

"We've also worked together to develop a list of adventures that we want to share as a couple," says Ellen. "Some of the goals we have accomplished together include purchasing a home, kayaking in the Sea of Cortez, attending a play at the Oregon Shakespeare Festival, and teaching a first-aid class together. Dreams we're looking forward to include raising a child, visiting the Ecuadorian rainforest, and learning to cook healthier meals."

"We use our meetings to periodically review our successes," says Jim. "It is also an opportunity to focus on where we are headed in our shared dreams. Setting goals together is going to be a forever kind of thing for us."

"In other words," says the waiter, "setting goals doesn't have to be a solo experience."

Gourmet Group Goal Setting

"If, like Jim and Ellen, you think that two heads can be better than one," says the waiter, "imagine what six heads can accomplish. Mark Zitter, Steve Edelson, and Dave Richardson are three friends of a six-member group. They get together once a year to discuss their goals. One thing they all have in common is that they are graduates of Stanford University's Business School."

"We've gotten together at a retreat for the last five years," says Mark. "It is an opportunity to see if we are getting what we want out of life. Often people don't think clearly enough about what they want in life. A large portion of our retreat involves thinking through goals, talking about them, and discussing ways to achieve them."

"In the past," says Dave, "I set goals in one or two specific areas, like graduating from college or getting a job. The focus was narrow. Now I realize that if I want to stay balanced, I have to set goals in a number of categories, such as work, financial, spiritual, health, and relationships."

"The biggest value of group goal setting," stresses Steve, "is the discipline. The process involves thinking about your goals, writing them down, reading them to the group, looking at them a year later, and revising them. Without the group, I don't think I would be as thorough."

"One of the motivators is accountability," says Dave. "You know you will be telling the group what you did. At first, I was concerned that this would lead to a competitive feeling. But it hasn't been a problem. There is encouragement in the group to be open and vulnerable. If anyone feels that we are trying to build ourselves up rather than to be open, we talk about it. I feel that I'm with a group of friends who care about me and would like to see me reach my goals. Support is important."

"Group goal setting can also help you gain perspective on your priorities," says Mark. "One of my goals was to spend more time with my father. I wanted to ask him questions about how he'd made some of his decisions when he was younger. We arranged a weekend of tennis in Vermont. Afterward, my Dad said he was flattered that his adult son would want to spend time with his old man. I enjoyed the time alone with him."

"Group goal setting also encourages you to clarify your goals," says Dave. "It may sound confusing to the group, but by explaining it to them, you make it clearer in your own mind."

"One of the unexpected benefits of our retreats," adds Steve, "is that in reviewing goals, you realize how fast life goes by. Like a near-death experience, it makes you want to live life more fully."

"If setting goals seems too cranium-oriented," says the waiter, "then maybe you will enjoy doing it with friends. Mark, Steve, and Dave find that setting goals along with traveling to a new location to meet, including play time between the meetings, and visiting a restaurant afterward makes for a pleasurable social experience."

An Irresistible Inventor

"Now let's hear from Sally Fox," says the waiter. "She's an inventor and an eco-aware entrepreneur. One of her goals may affect what you wear."

As Sally starts talking, you hear a smile in her voice. "My diary used to be a lot of chatter about how I feel. Then I started concentrating on things I was going after and articulations of my goals. Writing down goals formalizes them in your mind. Let me tell you about one of my biggest goals.

"After graduating with a degree in agricultural entomology, I worked with a cotton breeder. He had some seeds with brown instead of white lint. The beauty of the brown cotton caught my eye. In the textile industry, everyone knew about colored cotton, but the fiber was too short and weak to be spun on machines. My hobbies are spinning and weaving, so I started to experiment with the brown cotton. I planted seeds in little pots and cross-pollinated them with longer-fibered plants. At first, it was for fun to see if it could be done.

"My first big test plot was a half acre. The results from this plot were unexpected. Cotton breeders and the literature told me that I should get brown, tan, and white cotton. Instead, I got sixteen discernible colors. It was exciting. If the experts were so inaccurate at explaining what I saw, it meant that no one knew anything about this. At that point, I made it my goal to improve the fiber so it could be spun on commercial machines.

"I quit my job in San Diego and moved to Bakersfield, where I'd been offered a two-acre test plot. It was a scary move. I was giving up my income and moving alone to a remote place. I'd never been a farmer and I had to figure out everything for myself. In 1988, I grew enough cotton to run my first machine-spinning test. The test was a success.

"But big dreams can also meet big obstacles. One of my mistakes occurred in my first year of producing," says Sally. "A farmer held my cotton hostage.

"My early contracts weren't written clearly enough to protect me. A mill was ready to buy my cotton, but the farmer I'd contracted with to grow it wouldn't release it. He wanted more money. I figured if I didn't get the cotton to the mill, they might never do business with me again. So I decided, even if it was unfair that I lose all my profit to the farmer, it was more important that the cotton get to the customer.

"Most people personalize the first few obstacles they meet and give up," says Sally. "I try to learn from my mistakes. I think of that $30,000 loss to the grower as my MBA. The mill ended up liking my cotton so much that they wanted 2,000 acres of it. That represented a four-million-dollar contract back then.

"Imagine the possibilities," Sally says excitedly. "Colored cotton is environmentally efficient because you don't have to dye it. Eighty-five percent of the waste that a mill has to deal with is related to dyeing. My cotton saves the mill money. Colored cotton is also a more vigorous plant than white cotton. It needs fewer chemically-derived fertilizers, pesticides, and defoliants. We've also discovered that the color actually intensifies in the wash. And then there's the consumer. A sweater in the L.L. Bean catalog, made from a blend of my fiber, costs $39. The cheapest dyed cotton sweater in the catalog costs $42.

"I call my cotton Fox Fiber. It's used in products made by Land's End, Esprit, Seventh Generation, and Levi's. At present, my company, Natural Cotton Colours, has 6,000 acres in cultivation. My long-term goal is to replace dyed cotton. I think it will take about 100,000 acres. I dream of one day walking into a store and seeing khaki-colored pants, coyote brown shirts, and tan sweaters all made from Fox Fiber.

"Having goals has given me strength, the ability to stick with what is necessary, and the excitement to get others to share in my dream."

Just then the conductor returns to the dining car. "I trust you have had enough food for thought," says the conductor.

"Yes," you say. "It was quite nourishing."

A Reality Binder

"Good. Then I have a serious question. We've come only partway down the train. If you write down your dreams and are specific, there's a good chance you will improve your success at turning dreams into reality. You can get off the train here, or I can extend your ticket to show you something amazing. I can show you several more cars that will guarantee your success."

You nod enthusiastically.

"Excellent." The conductor snaps his fingers. You hear a whooshing sound and duck as something strange zooms over your head. It is a rainbow-colored binder. It flaps, squawking, around the car, eventually coming to rest on the conductor's shoulder like a well-trained parrot.

"Squaaaawk. Hello."

"What is that?"

"This is a reality binder." The conductor reaches up to scratch the binder's spine.

"How does a flying binder fit into guaranteeing that I can turn my dreams into reality?"

"You'll see," says the conductor. "But first, you need a non-flying three-ring binder and paper. When we are done, your binder will contain three items: a plus-and-minus chart, bridging questions, and a review sheet."

The rainbow-colored binder squawks and preens her pages in anticipation.

"Come along," says the conductor. "She doesn't get many people who make it this far."

You follow the flying binder down the corridor toward the next car.

A Plus-and-Minus Chart

"You might know our next passenger," says the conductor.

The single passenger sitting in the car is familiar. He's balding, except for a fringe of hippie-esque hair that hangs to his shoulder. His glasses are pure John Lennon.

"Why, he looks like Benjamin Franklin," you exclaim.

"He *is* Benjamin Franklin," replies the conductor.

"But that's impossible."

"Nothing is impossible. It just so happens we have Mr. Franklin as one of our riders-in-spirit."

"Are you the real Benjamin Franklin?" you inquire.

"You can wager a kite on it," says Mr. Franklin with a chuckle. "From your looks, you must be a new rider. In which case, our dear friend the conductor has brought you to me for a lesson in decision making."

"Decision making?"

"Yes. How else can you know which of your dreams to invest time in?" His eyebrows arch inquisitively. "I will not advise you on what to do, but I will tell you how to decide whether it is worthwhile to pursue a dream."

With a flourish, he stands up and clasps his hands behind his back. "What perplexes us in making a decision is the fact that you can have only one thought in your mind at a time. That makes it difficult to determine the pros and cons of an enterprise. Because you can entertain only a single thought at a time, if that thought is pro, the venture will seem attractive one moment. If it is con, your endeavor may seem risky the next moment. From moment to moment, your resolve swings like a pendulum between yea and nay. To overcome this uncertainty, I have devised a simple procedure."

With these words, Mr. Franklin waves to the preening binder, which promptly swoops to a rolltop desk. Snuggling down on the desk, the binder opens to give Mr. Franklin access to one of its pages. Mr. Franklin primes his quill pen in an ink pot and draws a line down the center of the page. On one side of the line he prints a plus, and on the other side, a minus.

"My method is to make two columns on a sheet of paper. Over one column, I put a plus sign." He underlines the plus. "Over the other, a minus sign." His stylus circles the minus. "Now over the next several days, I jot down the plusses and minuses of a particular goal in the appropriate columns as they come to me."

Mr. Franklin steps back and motions you in front of the desk. "Now let us pick a dream from your dream book and we shall apply the plus-and-minus equation to determine if the costs of pursuing this particular dream are reasonable."

"Well, I have this one goal," you say. "I want to be able to remember the names of twenty people at a business meeting or at a party."

"A laudable goal," says Mr. Franklin. "Now let's apply the equation."

With Mr. Franklin's encouragement, you write down all the benefits of being able to remember people's names. For instance, remembering people's names would help you feel more comfortable in social situations. This goes in the plus column.

Then you think of any negatives. One negative might be that you have to take a course, which takes time. You list this in the minus column. Your chart looks like this:

+	-
More comfortable in social situations	Need to take a memory course, which will take time
Get rid of that panicky feeling when I am supposed to know someone or need to introduce them	Taking a course will cost money
People will feel more positive toward me because they like their names to be remembered	
Helps build my social and business contacts	
People are more likely to remember my name if I remember theirs	
Will come across better because I can be myself	

"When you have identified all the pros and cons," says Mr. Franklin, "estimate their weights. Where a pro and a con seem equal, draw a line through each of them. If you find a single plus reason equal to two minuses, strike out all three. Now try it on your chart."

Your finished chart looks like this:

+	-
~~More comfortable in social situations~~	~~Need to take a memory course, which will take time~~
Get rid of that panicky feeling when I am supposed to know someone or need to introduce them	~~Taking a course will cost money~~
~~People will feel more positive toward me because they like their names to be remembered~~	
Helps build my social and business contacts	
~~People are more likely to remember my name if I remember theirs~~	
Will come across better because I can be myself	

"Plusses and minuses cannot be weighed with the precision of arithmetic," says Mr. Franklin. "Yet when I have everything before me, I can judge better and am less likely to take a rash step. Bear in mind that some decisions may have only a single plus or minus, but that one element may tilt everything for or against the end result.

"Now if you'll excuse me, I am working on my signature. If I ever again get a chance to sign a Constitution, I want my signature to look more impressive than John Hancock's."

The Bridging Questions

Suddenly, the train lurches violently. The squeal of iron against iron assails the ears. You find yourself clutching a seat to keep your balance. While the train is still skidding to a halt, the conductor confidently strides to the exit door. He motions for you to follow.

Soon you are standing outside next to the tracks. The sight is awesome. A huge canyon seems ready to swallow the train. The tracks dangle out over the abyss. The train is perched on the edge of the precipice.

"Hmmm," muses the conductor. "A bit of an obstacle."

"I'll say," you say. "It looks like this trip is over." Then you notice them. Thousands of sets of rusted train tracks stretch from the horizon. The land is covered by tracks. All of them come to a faltering stop at the lip of the canyon. "What is this place?" you ask.

"Oh, this canyon is notorious," says the conductor. "It stops a lot of trains from reaching their destinations. The canyon even has a name, *I don't know where to start.*"

"Well, I guess it's going to stop us too."

"Nonsense," snorts the conductor. Removing a silver whistle from his pocket, he puffs up his cheeks — and blows. But there is no shrill screech. The whistle plays the opening strains of the William Tell overture (more popularly known as the theme for the Lone Ranger). From one car jump five overall-clad workers. Bounding, hopping, and leaping, they make their way to one of the flatbed cars. The flatbed is covered by a tarp. As they pull back the canvas, a gleaming array of chrome struts flash in the sun. With the confidence of experience, they hoist the struts to their shoulders and carry them to the canyon lip.

As they pass by, the conductor introduces them. "This is Who, How, What, When, and Where. They are the best bridge-building team in the business. If anyone can get us over a difficulty, they can."

Warming to their work, the bridge builders move faster than a hummingbird in a hurry. In the rising dust, you can see the team assembling the girders into a bridge shaped like the words WHO, HOW, WHAT, WHEN, and WHERE. As each support is finished, a section of track is laid on the rapidly forming span.

"You see," says the conductor, "when bolted together, these five questions are marvelous for crossing

canyons. Even when that canyon is, *I don't know where to start.*

"In your reality binder, write the words WHO, HOW, WHAT, WHEN, and WHERE on a clean page. Make each question specific to your goal. Then answer them. This builds your bridge. In fact, it is one of the best ways to keep yourself laying track toward your destination."

The Robinson Crusoe of goal setting

"Could you give me an example of how to use these bridging questions?"

"Sure," says the conductor. He takes you to a small group of passengers who are watching the bridge builders at work. "I believe you already know Jim Wiltens?"

"Yes, I met him and Ellen back in the dining car," you say.

"Jim, please give our passenger an example of how these bridge builders work," says the conductor.

"Sure," says Jim. "Let me explain how I used these questions on a goal. One of my childhood dreams was fueled by reading books like *My Side of the Mountain*, *Swiss Family Robinson*, and *Robinson Crusoe*. I was fascinated by the idea of surviving in the wilds with hardly any supplies. In my dream book I wrote down that I wanted to be marooned on a deserted island off the coast of Canada. My only supplies would be three fishhooks, 20 feet of cord, five matches, a knife, and four gallons of drinking water. I wouldn't bring a sleeping bag, food, or a tent."

"Whoa," you ask, "what about a walkie-talkie or something if you got in trouble?"

"No safety net. The idea was to be totally self-sufficient."

"That sounds dangerous."

"Potentially, it was. The Canadian Coast Guard warned me that the island I had chosen was not some palm-treed tropical paradise. It was a rugged bit of rock that faces cold incoming Pacific storms like the prow of a ship. I admit, in the beginning, I had the kind of apprehension that can stop any trip. But I used Benjamin Franklin's plus-and-minus chart to decide that this was something I really wanted to do. Then I put the bridge-building questions to work. I simply wrote down who, how, what, when, and where, and left space under each word. These are some of the simple questions I asked to get started:

"Who can I talk to about islands off the Canadian Coast?

"How will I get out to the island I choose?

"What can I eat?

"When will I go?

"Where can I get nautical charts of the West Coast of Vancouver Island?

"Once I had written the questions, I set out to answer them. Would you like to see something interesting?"

You nod enthusiastically.

Jim snaps open his briefcase and removes a portable computer. "I keep my reality binder on a computer. When I find the answer to a question, I type the answer in. A computer makes it easy to keep detailed records of my answers." He presses some buttons and twiddles his mouse to open a file. "For example, under 'What can I eat?', I had listed mussels, but a little more research showed that mussels would be toxic at the time of year I was going, so I added that new information.

"Every time I encountered another canyon, I asked more questions. When I answered the question, I laid a piece of track toward my destination. It's like the bridge builders down there," Jim points to the acrobatic engineers. "They build their bridge one section at a time. Eventually, I reached a point where I felt I had answered enough questions to make it across any difficulties. My bridge was complete and I proceeded to go across it just like the little engine in the children's story book — 'I think I can, I think I can . . . I know I can.' "

"So you actually did it?" you ask.

"Yes. In 1992 a fishing boat marooned me on Edward King Island. As with most adventures, there were unexpected surprises. While exploring the island I discovered a large cave. It looked as if it would provide excellent shelter. I immediately became caveman interior designer, envisioning an aboriginal bedroom, spear closet, and paleolithic kitchen. But as my eyes adjusted to the dim light, I noticed a decaying cedar box in a corner of my stone-age condo. Rock fall had cracked the powder-dry boards of the lid. I edged over to it. Peering inside, I saw a human skeleton. What I'd found was an ancient Indian burial cave.

"Whenever I confronted new challenges on the island, I immediately shifted to using the questions, *who*, *how*, *what*, *when*, and *where*. If you keep these questions positive and focused on where you want to go, you will find solutions."

Made in Japan

The conductor nods approvingly. "You set your goal and then you ask the questions that will get you there. We've had a whole nation of riders on this particular train."

"A whole nation!" you say. "That must have been crowded."

"Yes," chuckles the conductor. "Are you old enough to remember when MADE IN JAPAN meant poor quality? Years ago, unless you wanted colorful paper umbrellas or a toy with a life span measured in days, you just didn't buy Japanese products. Then in the

'50s an American named Edward Deming was invited to Japan to teach quality control. A number of Japanese corporations were so inspired by him that they set a major goal. The word they use for this goal is *Kaizen*. It means to seek to make a small improvement every day toward higher quality.

"Companies like Toyota, Honda, and Matsushita began to ask 'How can we improve the quality of our products a tiny bit every day?' For example, soldering workers at a Matsushita television factory wanted to attain a defect rate of one mistake per 500,000 to 1,000,000 connections. That's pretty amazing for such a monotonous job, but asking the questions gave them a way to make the goal a reality. *Kaizen* is now one of the most commonly used words in Japan. It's in newspapers, on radio, and on television. Your bridge-building questions are small steps, like *Kaizen*, that bring you closer to your goal every day."

"Do you have to write down your steps to reach a goal? Couldn't you just think about it?" you ask.

The conductor thoughtfully strokes his beard. "Remember how you felt when we came up to this canyon?"

"It seemed pretty overwhelming. I felt like we weren't going to make it."

"Most beginning goal setters feel that way. A reality binder shoves that overwhelming feeling aside and replaces it with action. By breaking a goal into small steps it gets you going by doing. 'Doing' is important. When a locomotive is preparing to pull 200 tons of freight, the tender starts by shoveling one scoop of coal into the fire box. At first, not much happens. But as he continues to 'do' his job, a head of steam builds. He feels the cars inching forward. If the tender continues shoveling a scoop at a time, he soon feels the clackety-clack of his train high-balling down the track. The reality binder replaces that 'overwhelmed feeling' with action. It helps you develop momentum.

"Eventually you may do a lot of the binder work in your head, but beginners are more successful if they lay their first tracks on paper. The simple action of putting your questions and answers on paper is powerful action. The bigger your dreams, the more you will benefit from starting a reality binder. Even if you use your reality binder on only one goal, it will help you start to think like a successful goal setter."

You've listened intently to what the conductor has been saying, and you are surprised when you look up and realize that the bridge builders are finished. A plaque riveted to the newly constructed bridge reads:

**Trains reach destinations by crossing
one piece of track at a time:
ASK who, how, what, when, AND where,
AND THEN ANSWER THE QUESTIONS**

The Review Sheet

The colorful avian binder lands on the conductor's hat. Its pages flash *who*, *how*, *what*, *when*, and *where*.

"Oh oh," crows the binder.

The train has started moving. It looks as if you and the conductor will have to run to catch it. The binder grabs the conductor by the hat and, flapping frantically, carries the conductor toward the train. You dash after them. Legs pumping, heart pounding, and puffing like the locomotive you are chasing, you barely catch the rail of the caboose. As you haul yourself aboard, the binder deposits the conductor next to you on the caboose platform.

"Nice run," says the conductor. "That's where most people run out of steam."

Gasping for breath, you ask, "Whaaa. . . whaaa. . . whaaat do you mean?"

"Come inside," says the conductor. "Rather than tell you, let's see if you can figure out the last part of goal setting yourself."

The interior of the caboose is cool, especially after your run. Every inch of wall and floor space is papered with brightly colored calendars. Even the table and chairs are plastered with calendars.

Two passengers turn to face you.

"First let me introduce you to Koren Wong," says the conductor. "Koren, could you tell us about how you use goals?"

"I keep my goals written on a sheet in my datebook," says Koren. "I have it with me all the time. As a teacher, I sometimes have a really long day and I like to be able to see my goals to refresh myself." Koren sweeps a strand of jet black hair from her face.

"As a special education teacher, I work with children who have learning difficulties. I've found that disabilities like dyslexia are only part of their problems.

Many of them also have trouble understanding appropriate social behavior. For example, if they want a crayon that someone else is using, they just grab it. One of my written goals is to help these kids develop appropriate social skills.

"I use something I call a classroom economy system. To promote feelings of success, students receive a tangible reward for appropriate social skills. The system uses play money. Kids earn rewards for doing things like entering the class quietly, putting away their backpacks, placing their homework on my desk, and raising their hands."

"Can they use this money for anything?" you ask.

"Yes. There's a list of things they can exchange their money for. For instance, there is a bin with small items like pencils, or they can save for a more expensive reward, such as a class video or field trip. For big items, like a field trip, kids have to pool their money. This system teaches cooperation and how to wait for bigger rewards."

"Does it work?"

"I had one ten-year-old student who used to scream and use a lot of profanity. He might have sixty outbursts in an hour. Goals I wrote for him included using a classroom voice and using appropriate language. At first, he wasn't interested in the classroom economy system, but after watching the other children earn rewards, he decided he wanted to participate too.

Three months later, he might act out two or three times a day. Some days, there was no screaming and no profanity."

"That's great," you say. "What else do you do?"

"I make the students and their parents aware of improvements by sending notes home every day. There are three check boxes on the note: 'Had a good day,' 'Had an okay day,' and 'Had a hard day'. I set a baseline; for instance, if the child used to have sixty outbursts and went down to forty, that's an improvement — Had a good day. If the child improved only by going down to fifty-eight, that might be an okay day. If the child had a hundred outbursts, that would be a hard day."

"Hmmm," you think. "This teacher seems to have a lot of ways to help her kids know if they are meeting their goals. Tangible items like play money and the notes keep the kids aware of the goals and their progress."

The conductor interrupts your thoughts. "Now, let's talk to Dave Scott. Dave participates in one of the world's toughest competitive events, the triathlon. A triathlon involves swimming 2.5 miles, bicycling 112 miles, and then running 26 miles. Dave, could you tell us about goal setting in your life?"

"I reached a point in my career," says Dave, "where I felt the only way to stay competitive was to increase the length of my training. Eventually I was working out almost nine hours a day. That's when I started breaking down physically and mentally. Something had to change. Like other athletes, I kept a daily training log, but I decided to monitor my mental well-being instead of my times. I developed something I call my 'perceived feeling scale'. It goes from 1 to 5: 1 is crummy; 2 is okay; 3 is reasonably good; 4 is great; and 5 is fantastic! After every practice, I would use my perceived feeling scale and log how I felt. Using this scale, I cut my practice times in half and concentrated on achieving 5's. Previously if I had a poor workout, I focused on that one negative incident. With my new scale, I was focusing on my plusses rather than my minuses."

"It must have worked," says the conductor. "Dave is a six-time winner of the Hawaiian Iron Man Triathlon and former world-record holder at eight hours, one minute." The conductor looks at you intently. "Well?" he says.

"I think I understand," you reply. "Both Koren and Dave have a way to track their progress. Koren uses play money and notes. Dave keeps a log of his perceived feeling scale. They regularly review their progress."

"Excellent," says the conductor.

"Excellent," parrots the binder. Out drifts a page from the binder like a loose feather.

The conductor catches the sheet, and holds it up for you to see. "A calendar like this is one way to remember to review your progress. Some people hang their review calendar on the door to their bedroom so they will see it every day. At Deer Crossing Camp, a children's summer camp, there is a blackboard on which the campers write down each step they accomplish toward their individual goals.

"When you complete a goal, return to your dream book. Next to your accomplished goal, write the date and what you did. To make your success stand out, use a bright color of ink, or stick a gold star by it, or circle it. If you follow this process, you will soon find your dream book filled with completed goals."

A plaque over the door reads:

> **Trains are on time because engineers keep checking their watches:**
> **REVIEW YOUR PROGRESS**

Nuts And Bolts
Of Goal Setting

"Now to put it all together, follow me," says the conductor. You turn around and head back through all the cars you have already visited until you arrive at the engine. The fire box is roaring. Dials and gauges quiver with energy. "I'll leave you with our engineer," says the conductor. "She will explain the nuts and bolts of turning dreams into reality."

The engineer is wearing twilight blue overalls covered with sequins. She snaps her suspenders, sending up a cloud of glitter dust. Silver star glasses are balanced on her nose.

The engineer greets you, "Welcome to my train of thought. Turning a dream into reality means you have to hook up five cars. First, write down your goal. An alternative to words would be to draw a picture, or stick a photograph in your dream book. *Put five goals in your dream book right now.*

"Second, be as specific as possible. Pretend that you are asking someone else for this goal as a gift. Make your description clear enough that a gift giver would get you exactly what you want. If you need categories to get you started, *write down some things you want, some experiences you want, and some characteristics you want to develop in yourself.*

"Third, go back to your dream book and choose a dream that you'd like to make a reality. If you aren't certain whether you want to invest your time in a dream, *write down all the plusses and all the minuses* in your reality binder. Cross out the ones that seem pretty equal. Then see if the dream still seems worthwhile.

"If you are overwhelmed because achieving a dream seems like trying to build a transcontinental railway, break it down into smaller goals and put those in your dream book. For instance, if you want to go to college but you're only fourteen, set a goal to visit two or three colleges, or send for the colleges' catalogs. If you're an adult who hasn't exercised since the Jurassic period and your big goal is to run a marathon, make it a goal to walk around the block five times this week, or sign up for an exercise class at your community center, or buy some running shoes. It's a start. Put big and little goals in your dream book.

"Fourth, to get started on a goal, *ask the questions, who, how, what, when, and where*. Keep your questions positive and aimed in the direction you want to go. If you come to an obstacle, keep asking the questions to find a way over this barrier.

"Finally, *review your progress*. Keeping a calendar of your progress is one way of staying aware of where you are. When you reach a goal, open your dream book and write in a brilliant color of ink the date and what you did." The engineer hands you a piece of paper. "Here's the checklist I use to keep on track."

1. PUT YOUR GOAL ON PAPER

Write down your goal. Example: I want to learn to juggle.

_____

_____

2. BE SPECIFIC

Now rewrite your goal being as specific as possible. Example: I want to juggle three balls for fifteen seconds.

_____

_____

3. DECIDE WITH A PLUS-AND-MINUS CHART

The plus-and-minus chart helps you decide if you want to invest time in a particular goal. In the plus column, list positive benefits you get by accomplishing the goal. In the minus column, list drawbacks of going for the goal. For example, for the juggling goal, plusses might be increased coordination and being able to entertain friends. A minus might be that juggling takes time to learn.

+	−

4. ASK WHO, HOW, WHAT, WHEN, WHERE

Who do I . . . need help from, need to contact, need to convince . . .

How will I get the . . . time, money, confidence . . .

What resources do I need . . . books, education, money . .

When will I do it . . .

Where can I . . . do it, get what I need, find help. . .

5. REVIEW YOUR PROGRESS

Use a calendar to keep track of your progress toward your goal. Every day write down what you've done to take you towards your dream.

Mon	Tue	Wed	Thu	Fri	Sat	Sun

"Do me a favor," says the engineer. "Fold your arms across your chest."

You fold your arms.

"Look at which arm crosses on top," says the engineer, touching that arm. "Remember that arm. Now separate your arms and try again."

You cross your arms a second time.

"See how you've put the same arm on top? Now, cross your arms quickly, but this time switch the arm that is on top."

You try it. "It feels awkward."

"Aha," says the engineer. "You see, you have a habit."

You look at her in consternation.

"A long time ago you started crossing one arm over the other, or slipping your left arm in your jacket before your right, or tying your shoes with a certain knot," says the engineer. "These are habits you feel comfortable with. You don't even have to think about them. If you start a dream book and a reality binder, you will develop another habit. A good habit that will take you a long way in life."

Have a good trip.

About The Author

From the dream book of Jim Wiltens:

√   Own and operate a wilderness summer camp
√   Attain a black belt in the martial arts
      Rescue seals that have become entangled in fishing
              line
√   Learn to prepare sushi
√   Publish a book on edible and poisonous plants
√   Become a certified emergency medical technician
      Dive on a sunken galleon and recover treasure
√   Become a nationally published cartoonist
      Take a class in celestial navigation
√   Buy a townhouse
√   Write a book for teens and parents on motivation
√   Do 1,000 consecutive sit-ups
      Catch arrows shot from a thirty-five pound bow
√   Conduct SCUBA classes for teens in Hawaii
√   Publish a book on goal setting
√   Juggle four balls for fifteen seconds

Learn to switch back and forth between the following
    dialects and accents: Cockney, German,
    Scottish, Brooklyn, Russian, British, and
    French

Skipper a sailboat from California to Hawaii

√   Interview Wozniak, inventor of the Apple computer

Memorize the names of twenty-five parents taking one
    of my one-night classes

√   Become a rescue sheriff

√   Learn twenty-five words in American Sign Language

√   Touch a whale

√   Kayak white water in the jungles of South America

(Checked items have been accomplished.)

Jim Wiltens has worked as a marine biologist, analytical chemist, university coach of championship water polo teams, and award-winning writer. As a one-time swimmer and water polo player, he competed at national and international levels.

Jim loves a good adventure. He has snorkeled with giant squid, climbed active volcanoes, explored sunken wrecks, and prospected for gold. Tales of his adventures have appeared in numerous publications. He is co-owner and director of Deer Crossing Camp, a wilderness summer camp dedicated to bringing out the best qualities in children.

Jim speaks about goal setting, motivation, and self-esteem enhancement to parenting groups, school assemblies, teacher in-services, and corporate groups.

If you would like information about Jim Wiltens' talks and seminars, write:

Deer Crossing Press
P.O. Box 60517
Sunnyvale, CA 94088–0517

For information about Deer Crossing Camp, write or call:

Deer Crossing Camp
1919 Ridge Rd.
Mokelumne Hill, CA 95245
(209) 293-2328
www.deercrossingcamp.com

 **Nagging,
Nit-picking,
& Nudging**

A guide to motivating, inspiring, and influencing kids aged 10-18

Jim Wiltens is to the parents of teens what Dr. Spock was for so many years to the parents of babies.
Bay Area Parent Magazine

____ Copies pbk. $9.95

The five secrets of goal-setting success

This book will benefit anyone who wants to do more than dream about life's adventures.
John Goddard. First explorer to kayak the entire Nile river

____ Copies pbk. $9.95

Please send ____ books x $9.95/book   = ____

Postage and handling ($1.75 for first book plus $1.00 for each additional copy).   = ____

California residents add sales tax of 72¢/book.   = ____

Make check or money order payable to *Deer Crossing Press*. No cash or CODs please.   Total = ____

Mail books to:

Name: _____

Address: _____

City: _____ State: ___ Zip: _____

Phone: (_____) _____

Send this form with your payment to:

Deer Crossing Press

Su 690 Emerald Hill Rd.
Redwood City, CA 94061   **7**